BIBLE TRIVIA

Questions & Answers from the Bible

BARBOUR BOOKS

An Imprint of Barbour Publishing, Inc.

© MCMXCVIII by Barbour Publishing, Inc.

ISBN 1-59789-079-0

Published by Barbour Publishing, Inc., P.O. Box 719, Uhrichsville,
Ohio 44683, www.barbourbooks.com

 Member of the
Evangelical Christian
Publishers Association

Printed in the United States of America.

5 4 3 2 1

THE CREATION AND THE FALL
Genesis 1–10

1.) Who wrote the book of Genesis?

2.) What did God do on the first day?

3.) What three things did God create on the fourth day to light the universe?

4.) Did you know that gold and onyx could be found in the Garden of Eden? (Genesis 2:12)

5.) Why did Eden have a river running through it?

6.) The name of the first man was:
   a) Abraham
   b) Noah
   c) Joseph
   d) Adam

7.) Who named all of the living creatures?

8.) Why did God decide to create a woman?

9.) The name of the first woman was:
   a) Evelyn
   b) Rachel
   c) Eve
   d) Rebekah

10.) Did you know that the first woman's name means mother of all living? (Genesis 3:20)

11.) What did God take from Adam to make Eve?

12.) Did you know that Adam and Eve were the first married couple? (Genesis 2:23–24)

13.) The first woman was tempted by a:
   a) serpent
   b) ladybug
   c) dinosaur
   d) spider

14.) If Eve would eat the forbidden fruit, the serpent promised her:

    a) clothing
    b) riches
    c) a starring role in a movie
    d) knowledge of good and evil

15.) Did you know that Moses wrote the first five books of the Bible?

16.) After discovering their nakedness, how did Adam and Eve clothe themselves?

17.) What did Adam and Eve do when they heard God calling?

18.) When he was caught disobeying God, Adam blamed:

    a) the serpent
    b) bad programs on television
    c) Cain
    d) Eve

? ? ? ? ? ? ? ?

19.) After Adam and Eve ate the forbidden fruit, God:
   a) sent them out of Eden
   b) let them stay in Eden
   c) poured manna from heaven
   d) told them to build an ark so he could begin the human race again

20.) Whom did God put in place to guard the tree of life?

21.) Did you know that the first five books of the Bible are called the Pentateuch?

THE FIRST MURDER/THE FLOOD
Genesis 4–10

1.) Who was the first son of Adam and Eve?

2.) Who was the second son born to Adam and Eve?

3.) Did you know that the slaying of Abel by Cain was the first murder?

4.) When Cain went out of the Lord's presence, he went to live in:
   - a) Mod
   - b) Nod
   - c) Sod
   - d) Cod

5.) Did you know that John Steinbeck wrote a book called *East of Eden?* This is also where Cain went to live after being exiled. (Genesis 4:16)

6.) Who was Cain and Abel's brother?

7.) Who was Methuselah's father?

8.) What is mentioned twice about Enoch?

9.) Methuselah lived how many years?
- a) 30
- b) 69
- c) 90
- d) 969

10.) God told Noah to build:
- a) a yacht for Christian cruises
- b) an airplane
- c) an ark
- d) a tugboat

11.) Did you know that a cubit measures 18 inches long?

12.) How old was Noah when the flood began?

13.) One of Noah's sons was named:
- a) Ham
- b) Sham
- c) Salami
- d) Pastrami

14.) Did you know that Noah's ark was 450 feet long?

15.) What are the first five books of the Bible called?

A NEW WORLD
Genesis 11–50

1.) To reach heaven, the people tried to build:
- a) the Empire State Building
- b) a highway to heaven
- c) the Tower of Babel
- d) the Sears Building

2.) What did the Lord do when He discovered that men were trying to build a tower to reach heaven?

3.) Did you know that archaeologists discovered towers built to worship false gods in Mesopotamia?

4.) What land did Lot choose for himself when he and Abram separated?

5.) Did you know that Mohammed, the founder of the religion of Islam, was from the line of Ishmael?

6.) Hagar was:
   a) the mother of Ishmael
   b) the founder of the Haggar Clothing Company
   c) the mother of Abraham
   d) Sarah's neighbor

7.) When Ishmael was born, his father Abram was age:
   a) 26
   b) 36
   c) 86
   d) 96

8.) Abram's name was changed to:
   a) Lot
   b) Abraham
   c) Bam-Bam
   d) Brahma

9.) Why did God change Abram's name to Abraham?

? ? ? ? ? ? ? ?

10.) Did you know that the Hebrew word "Shaddai" is the name used for God most often in the Bible's early books?

11.) Did you know that Shaddai means "All Sufficient" or "Almighty"?

12.) Who wrote the first five books of the Bible?

13.) When God promised Abraham that his wife Sarah would have a baby, he:
   a) praised God
   b) invested in a college fund
   c) bought a box of expensive cigars
   d) laughed

14.) Why did Abraham give God such a response to the news?

15.) God destroyed the evil cities of:
   a) Sodom and Gomorrah
   b) Bethlehem and Nazareth
   c) London and Paris
   d) Bug Tussle and Navel Lint

16.) What happened to Lot's wife when she looked back at the cities?

17.) What was the name of Lot's wife?
   a) Marilyn Monroe
   b) Marlene Deitrich
   c) Mary Magdelene
   d) Her name is not recorded in the Bible.

18.) Did you know that the ruins of the two cities probably lie underneath the waters of the Dead Sea?

19.) Abraham and Sarah didn't want their son Isaac to marry any of the local women because they were:
   a) Canaanites
   b) Israelites
   c) members of the Electric Light Orchestra
   d) ugly

? ? ? ? ? ? ? ? ?

20.) Abraham's servant gave Rebekah:
- a) a happy meal
- b) Jewel Mermaid Midge
- c) silver jewelry
- d) gold jewelry

21.) How long did Jacob serve Laban before he could marry Rachel?

22.) Who was Joseph's father?

23.) Joseph's father loved him more than any of his other children because Joseph:
- a) was the child of his old age
- b) was handsome
- c) had good taste in clothes
- d) showered him with gold, frankincense, and myrrh

24.) What did Joseph's father make for Joseph?

25.) Joseph's brothers hated him even more after Joseph dreamed that:
   a) there would be a famine
   b) his brothers would serve Joseph
   c) his brothers would invent the paper clip
   d) Joseph would be the lead singer of the Partridge Family

26.) What did Joseph do during the years when there was plenty of food?

27.) What is the last event recorded in Genesis?
   a) Joseph's death
   b) Abraham's death
   c) Sarah's death
   d) Rebekah's death

? ? ? ? ? ? ? ?

ONE BIG EXIT
Exodus 1–37

1.) Who wrote the book of Exodus?

2.) Did you know that the word "Exodus" is from the Greek meaning "exit"?

3.) The Israelites in Egypt were:
    a) used car salesmen
    b) slaves
    c) Pharoahs
    d) rock stars

4.) The Israelites built for the Egyptians:
    a) the Tower of Babel
    b) a synagogue
    c) the Eiffel Tower
    d) treasure cities

5.) Who found the baby Moses?

6.) Where was Pharoah's daughter when she found Moses?

7.) Did you know that Moses' name is Egyptian rather than Hebrew? Egyptian Pharoahs Ramoses (Rameses) and Thutmose (Thothmes) had similar names.

8.) Moses saw an angel of God in a:
   a) microwave oven
   b) camp fire
   c) burning bush
   d) Christmas tree

9.) God promised the Israelites:
   a) forty acres and a mule
   b) a land flowing with milk and honey
   c) straw for bricks
   d) a land flowing with soda pop and potato chips

10.) Because of God's power, what could Moses turn his rod into?

? ? ? ? ? ? ? ? ?

11.) During the plagues, God turned the water of the River Nile into:
   a) blood
   b) wine
   c) milk and honey
   d) all the soda they could drink

12.) Did you know that the plagues were aimed against the false gods of Egypt? For example, the plague of darkness (Exodus 10:21–23) was against Ra, the Egyptian sun god.

13.) Before the Israelites left Egypt, God told them to ask for:
   a) manna
   b) milk and honey
   c) thirty shekels each
   d) silver and gold

14.) What is the Jewish observance to remember God's angel passing over their houses?

15.) What great miracle did God perform through Moses as the Israelites left Egypt?

16.) The first five books of the Bible were written by:
   a) Ezekiel
   b) Jesus
   c) Bruce Bannon
   d) Moses

17.) Were the Israelites expected to gather manna on the Sabbath?

18.) Why did God rain meat down on the wilderness?

19.) God rained what kind of meat on the wilderness for the Israelites?
   a) pigs
   b) shrimp
   c) quail
   d) cats and dogs

20.) On Mt. Sinai, God gave Moses:
- a) the Sermon on the Mount
- b) the Ten Commandments
- c) the Olivet Discourse
- d) manna

21.) Moses' brother was named:
- a) Aaron
- b) Joseph
- c) Fatty Z
- d) Tamar

22.) While Moses was away on Mt. Sinai, the Israelites made:
- a) gold jewelry
- b) a golden calf
- c) the first television set
- d) an army tank for protection

23.) The first five books of the Bible are called the:
- a) Pentagon
- b) Hexagon
- c) Octagon
- d) Pentateuch

24.) What other food did God provide?

25.) Who guarded the mercy seat?

STRONGMAN SAMSON
Judges 13–16

1.) Where in the Bible does Samson's story appear?

2.) What group of people ruled Israel when the book was written?

3.) Did you know that an angel appeared to Samson's mother before his birth and told her that his hair was not to be cut?

4.) The angel also told Samson's mother not to drink:
   a) 7-up
   b) manna
   c) water from the creek
   d) wine or strong drink

5.) The angel also appeared before:
   a) Samson's father Manoah
   b) Noah
   c) Herman Munster
   d) Fred Flintstone

6.) What was the angel's name?

7.) The woman Samson wanted to marry was a:
 a) Jewess
 b) Hollywood star
 c) U.S. citizen
 d) Philistine

8.) When a lion attacked Samson after he visited the woman, he:
 a) killed it with his bare hands
 b) killed it with a slingshot
 c) made it his pet and named it Delilah
 d) ran over it with his car

9.) Inside the lion's carcass, Samson found:
 a) the sword Excalibur
 b) raspberry flavored spring water
 c) a swarm of bees and honey
 d) granola bars

? ? ? ? ? ? ? ?

10.) What did Samson challenge his wedding banquet guests to do?

11.) The answer was given away by:
    a) an angel
    b) Samson's wife
    c) Samson's mother
    d) the TV news

12.) Because she thought Samson hated her, after the feast Samson's wife married:
    a) Samson's friend
    b) Abraham
    c) Adam
    d) Michael Card

13.) Did you know that Samson was the thirteenth judge?

14.) Samson killed a thousand Philistines with a:
    a) dog's tail
    b) bucket of cream pies
    c) bb gun
    d) donkey's jawbone

15.) What did Samson do to make good on his promise to give thirty people fine cloaks?

16.) After the battle, God gave Samson water from:
   a) a rock
   b) the Old Faithful geyser at Yellowstone National Park
   c) a vending machine that appeared inside of a burning bush
   d) the donkey's jawbone

17.) In exchange for betraying Samson, the Philistine lords offered Delilah:
   a) 1100 pieces of silver each
   b) a nose ring
   c) a pet lizard
   d) two large ruby rings for her toes

? ? ? ? ? ? ? ?

18.) Did you know that Samson judged Israel for twenty years? (Judges 15:20)

19.) Did you know that if the lords were offering Delilah silver shekels, they were willing to pay about $700 each to learn about Samson?

20.) At first, Samson told Delilah that he would be weak if he were:
- a) shaven
- b) made to fast for three days
- c) were tied with seven green cords of rope
- d) were forced to drink nothing but fruit juice for three weeks

21.) The second time, Samson told her that he had to be tied with:
- a) silly string
- b) green yarn
- c) new rope that had never been used
- d) pieces of construction paper

22.) What did Samson tell Delilah the third time?

23.) What happened each time Samson lied to Delilah?

24.) After Samson lied to her, Delilah:
   a) gave up
   b) pestered Samson every day to tell her until he confessed
   c) lied to the Philistine lords and collected her money
   d) subbed for Vanna White as a letter turner on "Wheel of Fortune"

25.) After Samson was captured by the Philistines, what happened to his shaven hair?

26.) Did you know that Samson's head was never to be shaven because he was a Nazarite?

27.) Samson got into this trouble because he:

    a) hung out with the school bullies
    b) was no longer walking with the Lord
    c) wanted Israel to have a king
    d) was out of money

28.) Why were the Philistines gathered to honor their god?

29.) How many Philistines were present at the gathering?

30.) At the gathering, Samson:

    a) told Delilah she would never have children
    b) prayed to God for strength
    c) decided to worship the god Dagon
    d) became a member of the Lions Club

31.) What happened when God granted Samson's request?

RUTH

1.) Do we know who wrote the book of Ruth?

2.) Did you know that Ruth's story took place about the same time as the book of Judges?

3.) The family left home because:
   a) the wife had turned into a pillar of salt
   b) they had charged too much on their credit cards
   c) there wasn't any strawberry bubble gum in their local stores
   d) there wasn't enough food to eat because of famine

4.) Naomi and her family went to:
   a) Moab
   b) Boaz
   c) Boz
   d) Boomtown

5.) Where were Naomi and her family from?

6.) Which daughter-in-law stayed with Naomi?

7.) The women Naomi's sons married were named:
   a) Oprah Winfrey and Sally Jesse Raphael
   b) Orpah and Ruth
   c) Opie and Babe Ruth
   d) Mary and Martha

8.) How long did they live in Moab before both of Naomi's sons died?

9.) After her sons died, Naomi decided to:
   a) start a computer consulting business
   b) open a store called Naomi's Notions
   c) stay in Moab
   d) return to her homeland

10.) After making her plans, Naomi told her daughters-in-law to:
  a) go back and live with their mothers
  b) go into business with her
  c) take care of her in her old age
  d) to be sure to raise her grand-children right

11.) What happened to Naomi's husband?

12.) Did you know that the Moabites worshiped false gods? Orpah and Ruth were Moabites. Naomi told Ruth to return to her gods. (Ruth 1:15)

13.) What did Ruth offer to do if Naomi would let her stay?
  a) give her a new car every year until her death
  b) keep house for her
  c) find Naomi a new husband
  d) convert to Judaism

14.) When Naomi and Ruth arrived in Bethlehem, Naomi:
  a) changed her name to Mara
  b) got a new Social Security number
  c) burned incense to Jehovah
  d) told everyone that they were following a star

15.) What grain was being harvested in Bethlehem when they arrived?

16.) What did Ruth do to provide food?

17.) Did you know that gleaning is the process of gathering up the leftover harvest in the fields? God's law allowed for the poor to glean the fields for their food. (Lev 19:9–10)

18.) Boaz was a relative of:
  a) Naomi's husband
  b) Ruth
  c) Orpah
  d) Boyz to Men

19.) In return for gleaning only in his field, Boaz promised Ruth:

    a) that she would be safe and have plenty of water to drink

    b) three nose rings and a snake tattoo

    c) that she would be declared the most beautiful woman in Bethlehem

    d) that she could return to Moab

20.) Boaz was kind to Ruth because she:

    a) was a great beauty

    b) would soon inherit a fortune

    c) had won a $10,000,000 sweepstakes

    d) had taken good care of Naomi

21.) What two grains did Ruth glean?

22.) Does the Bible reveal the name of the kinsman Boaz told Ruth about?

23.) After the harvest season, Naomi told Ruth to:
   a) ask Boaz what to do next
   b) glean rye
   c) open a bakery since they had so much grain
   d) wear sackcloth since they would soon starve

24.) Boaz gave Ruth:
   a) six measures of barley
   b) the book "365 Ways to Serve Barley"
   c) a lecture on laziness
   d) the three nose rings and tattoo he had promised earlier

25.) What did Boaz buy on behalf of Naomi and Ruth?

26.) The kinsman wouldn't buy it because:
   a) Naomi was a Moabite
   b) Ruth was a Moabite
   c) he was a Moabite
   d) he didn't have enough money

27.) After Boaz bought the property, the elders decided to:

    a) accept Ruth as one of their own

    b) stone Ruth

    c) send her information about investments

    d) encourage her to take the money and go to college

28.) After the purchase, Boaz:

    a) asked Ruth for 10% of the money

    b) suggested that they go into the real estate business together

    c) married Ruth

    d) sent Ruth back to Moab

29.) Did you know that the son of Ruth and Boaz was to be King David's grandfather?

30.) How many books are in the Bible?

THE FAITHFUL MOTHER

I Samuel 1–3

1.) Did you know that I and II Samuel are considered one book in the Hebrew Bible?

2.) Hannah was upset because:
   - a) she had no children
   - b) she had no husband
   - c) she had thrown away her entry to a $10,000,000 sweepstakes
   - d) she was out of lipstick

3.) What did Hannah request of the Lord?

4.) If God answered her prayer, Hannah promised:
   - a) to become a Benedictine nun
   - b) that her son would belong to God
   - c) that she would divorce her husband
   - d) that she would go for the perfect attendance pin at church

5.) Hannah also promised the Lord that her son's hair would never be:
   a) dyed red
   b) tied with purple ribbons
   c) washed
   d) cut

6.) How did God answer Hannah's prayer?

7.) Did you know that Hannah named her son Samuel because she had asked God for him?   (I Samuel 1:20)

8.) Hannah took her child to:
   a) Eli the priest
   b) Nazareth
   c) her husband
   d) an Amy Grant concert

9.) Did you know that a bullock is a young bull? Hannah's family sacrificed a bullock to the Lord before giving Samuel over to Eli the priest. (I Samuel 1:25)

10.) Why did Hannah give up her child?

11.) The sons of Eli the priest were:
   a) handsome
   b) winners of the Star Search
      contest
   c) evil
   d) kings

12.) As he grew, Samuel:
   a) ministered before the Lord
   b) asked to eat rich foods
   c) wanted to be more important
      than Abraham
   d) aced both calculus and
      trigonometry

13.) Each year, Hannah made Samuel a:
   a) loaf of bread
   b) videotape of all the family
      events he was missing
   c) little coat
   d) coat of many colors

14.) Eli the priest:
- a) blessed Hannah and her husband Elkanah
- b) made Hannah the first woman priest
- c) gave Hannah a special portion of food
- d) promised Hannah's husband tickets to the Super Bowl

15.) How many times did the Lord call Samuel before Samuel answered the Lord "Speak; for thy servant heareth"?

16.) Did Hannah have more children after Samuel?

17.) Did you know that Hannah was blessed by the Lord with three sons and two daughters?   (I Samuel 2:21)

18.) What did God say would happen to Eli's sons?

19.) The Lord had this plan for Eli's sons because they were:
- a) evil
- b) next in line to become priests
- c) ruddy and handsome
- d) good

20.) Instead of letting Eli's sons be priests, God planned to:
- a) send Samuel to Ninevah
- b) have Samuel and Eli swallowed by a big fish
- c) shower riches and fame on Eli
- d) raise up His own priest who would do His will

21.) When God spoke to Samuel, Samuel thought he was being called by:
- a) Eli
- b) Hannah
- c) an angel
- d) the alien E.T.

22.) When Samuel was called by the Lord, Eli was:

    a) sleeping

    b) watching a prime-time soap opera

    c) trimming his toenails

    d) sacrificing a ram

23.) The Lord told Samuel He planned to:

    a) bless Eli

    b) bless Eli's sons

    c) allow Eli to win a dream house in a raffle

    d) punish Eli's house because Eli's sons were evil

? ? ? ? ? ? ? ?

24.) After the Lord spoke to Samuel, everyone knew Samuel would be a:
    a) lawyer
    b) prophet
    c) vegetarian
    d) hippie

25.) Did you know that the first book of
Samuel was written in the tenth
century before Christ?

FROM JUDGES TO A KING
I Samuel 8-10

1.) Did you know that God's people were under a government called a theocracy? That means they were ruled by God.

2.) When Samuel got old, he:
   a) married a young woman
   b) made his sons judges in his place
   c) had to take antacid after every meal
   d) refused to stop judging Israel

3.) The people were unhappy with Samuel's sons because they:
   a) took bribes and did not rule fairly
   b) did not exercise
   c) had promised free education for all and then didn't build any schools
   d) had not kept their promise of giving everyone a chicken in every pot

4.) What were the names of Samuel's two sons?

5.) Had Samuel been a good judge?

6.) Did you know that Samuel was the last of the true judges of Israel?

7.) When the people demanded a king, Samuel:
  - a) was pleased
  - b) prayed to the Lord
  - c) gave everyone a chicken
  - d) promised everyone free health benefits

8.) The Lord told Samuel to:
  - a) let the people see how a king would rule
  - b) sacrifice two goats and a perfect male ram
  - c) produce two more sons more worthy to be judges
  - d) store grain for seven years because there would be seven years of famine

9.) When the people asked for a king, whom did the Lord say they were really rejecting?

10.) Samuel warned the people that a king would be:
   a) greedy
   b) a blessing to the nation
   c) as brilliant as Albert Einstein
   d) as rich as Bill Gates

11.) Did the people heed Samuel's warning?

12.) What was the name of Israel's first king?

13.) Did you know that Saul was a descendant of the tribe of Benjamin? Saul's father was Kish; his grandfather was Abiel; his great-grandfather was Zeror, and his great-great grandfather was a powerful Benjamite named Aphiah.

? ? ? ? ? ? ? ? ?

14.) Saul was known for:
   a) owning a red monster truck
   b) winning the pie eating contest at the state fair five years in a row
   c) being the shortest and ugliest man in all of Israel
   d) being the tallest and most handsome man in all of Israel

15.) Saul and his servant were traveling through the country trying to find:
   a) his father's lost donkeys
   b) a Motel 6
   c) a wife for Saul
   d) jobs modeling men's fashions for the Israeli edition of B.C. Man

16.) Did you know that Saul and his servant planned to pay Samuel one fourth of a silver shekel, or about 18 cents, to tell them where they could find what they were seeking? (I Samuel 9:8)

17.) Samuel knew Saul was to be the king because:

    a) God had written the message on the wall

    b) God had told Samuel in his ear that Saul was the one

    c) Samuel could feel it in his bones

    d) Samuel's left big toe always ached when he saw a king

18.) Saul was surprised that Samuel spoke to him with respect because Saul:

    a) was normally treated as stupid because he was handsome

    b) had not had a bath in three days

    c) only had 18 cents

    d) was from the smallest of the twelve tribes of Israel and his family was not important

? ? ? ? ? ? ? ?

19.) What did Samuel tell Saul about his father's lost donkeys?

20.) What did Samuel do after feeding Saul dinner?

21.) Whom did they ask where to find Samuel?

22.) Did you know that another name for a prophet is a seer? (I Samuel 9:9)

23.) After Saul met the company of prophets, he had the gift of:
   a) thirty silver shekels
   b) prophecy
   c) two nose rings
   d) a chain link fence to keep his father's donkeys from getting lost again

24.) Did everyone know right away that Saul was their new king?

YOUNG BLOOD

I Samuel 15–17

1.) Why did God reject Saul as king?

2.) Did you know that God sent Samuel to Bethlehem, the city of Jesus' birth, to find the next king? (I Samuel 16:4)

3.) Samuel thought that Eliab should be the second king because Eliab was:
   a) handsome
   b) rich
   c) planning to give Samuel money for his ministry
   d) good

4.) The Lord told Samuel that people see outward beauty, but He sees their:
   a) intelligence
   b) possessions
   c) time put in at Bible study class
   d) hearts

5.) Who was the future king's father?

6.) How many sons did Samuel see before he saw the future king?

7.) David was:
   a) short and slightly pudgy
   b) glowing with health and handsome to look at
   c) quarterback on the football team
   d) a brainy person who wore thick glasses

8.) What did the Lord tell Samuel to do when Samuel saw David?

9.) Why did Saul want to be soothed by music?

10.) David was skillful at playing the:
   a) electric organ
   b) kazoo
   c) accordion
   d) harp

11.) Who was to be the new king of Israel?

12.) Did you know that David was the youngest son of Jesse?

13.) In Saul's court, David:
    a) loved Saul and became his armor-bearer
    b) hated Saul because David wanted to be king right away
    c) became Saul's food taster
    d) was thrown into a lion's den

14.) Who was Goliath?

15.) Did you know that Goliath's height measured six cubits and a span? A cubit measures about 21 inches, while a span measures the length of three palms of a man's hand. This means that Goliath was over 11 feet tall. (I Samuel 17:4)

? ? ? ? ? ? ? ? ?

16.) Which of David's brothers went with Saul to battle the Philistines?

17.) While his brothers were in battle, young David:
   a) looked for his father's lost donkeys
   b) spent three days in the belly of a big fish
   c) tried out for his school's basketball team
   d) fed his father's sheep in Bethlehem

18.) How many days did Goliath taunt the Israelites?

19.) David's father sent him to visit the army to:
   a) take them food
   b) battle Goliath
   c) supply them with more bullets for their guns
   d) play the harp

20.) When David visited the army, he heard:
- a) a rousing version of "Three Blind Mice"
- b) the song "Taps" to bid the army good night
- c) an old-fashioned revival meeting
- d) Goliath's challenge to the army

21.) The person who killed Goliath was sure to get:
- a) a two-week vacation in the Bahamas
- b) a beating from Saul
- c) riches, Saul's daughter, and freedom
- d) nothing

22.) When David saw Saul, he offered to:
- a) play a polka on his harp
- b) write a new song just for Saul
- c) fight Goliath
- d) tend Saul's sheep

? ? ? ? ? ? ? ?

23.) To convince Saul he should fight, David said he had:

    a) won the Mr. Bodybuilder of Israel contest the previous year

    b) been the spokesman for Strong Arm Vitamins for ten years

    c) killed a lion and a bear who tried to steal his father's sheep

    d) eaten honey from the carcass of a lion who had attacked his father's sheep

24.) Whom did David think would allow him to win the battle?

25.) How many smooth stones did David select for his slingshot?

26.) The moment Goliath saw David, Goliath:

    a) ran away in fear

    b) made fun of David

    c) decided to worship the Lord

    d) asked him for skin care tips

27.) David told Goliath that he would kill Goliath and:
- a) appear on "America's Most Wanted"
- b) that Goliath would be on "Rescue 911"
- c) everyone would know about God
- d) that David would finally get a modeling job

28.) Did you know that even though David was armed with several stones, he only used one to cause Goliath to fall to the earth? (I Samuel 17:49)

29.) What did the Philistines do after David killed Goliath?

30.) What was Eliab's reaction to seeing David at the battlefront?

? ? ? ? ? ? ? ? ?

THE KINGS RULE
I Kings, Chapter 1

1.) Did you know that First and Second Kings were originally one book?

2.) What is King David like at the beginning of the first book of Kings?

3.) Adonijah was:
   a) David's father
   b) Bathsheba's son
   c) Solomon's older half-brother
   d) Solomon's stepson

4.) Adonijah declared that:
   a) he would be the next king
   b) all of his earnings would go to the homeless
   c) Israel would go back to being ruled by judges after King David's death
   d) it was time for the palace to be completely redecorated

5.) Did you know that Adonijah was David's oldest living son? The eldest son usually inherited his father's position.

6.) Did King David tell Adonijah that he would not be the next king?

7.) Adonijah was very:
   a) handsome
   b) homely
   c) nerdy
   d) geeky

8.) Who was Solomon's mother?

9.) The prophet Nathan told Solomon's mother to:
   a) speak to King David about Adonijah
   b) sacrifice a goat and two doves to the Lord
   c) burn peppermint incense until dawn
   d) crash the party

10.) Nathan was alarmed because:

    a) he hadn't eaten for two days

    b) there was to be a famine in the land

    c) he and Adonijah had argued

    d) Solomon was supposed to be the next king, not Adonijah

11.) Did King David know that Adonijah was ruling?

12.) Adonijah knew he was trying to take the throne without permission because he had not invited whom to the banquet?

13.) Did you know that Adonijah was attempting a *coup d'etat? A coup d'etat* occurs when someone takes power over a country without permission. Sometimes power is taken by force and results in war. Adonijah was trying to take power without fighting. This is called a bloodless coup.

14.) When King David heard that Adonijah was ruling, he:
   a) had Solomon anointed and declared king
   b) shrugged and said *"C'est la vie"*
   c) lifted his scepter and said, *"Carpe Diem"*
   d) demanded that Adonijah's head be brought to him on a plate

15.) What animal did Solomon ride to Gihon?

16.) To celebrate, they blew a:
   a) trumpet
   b) flute
   c) piccolo
   d) kazoo

17.) Who told Adonijah the news that Solomon had been declared king?

? ? ? ? ? ? ? ?

18.) Jonathan told Adonijah and his guests that Solomon had been blessed by:
- a) Bathsheba
- b) King David
- c) Solomon
- d) the Maytag repairman

19.) How did Jonathan know this?

20.) When the guests heard the news, they:
- a) blessed Adonijah
- b) blessed Solomon
- c) asked Adonijah for doggy bags of food to take home
- d) rose up and left the party in fear

21.) After hearing the news, Adonijah:
- a) begged King Solomon not to kill him
- b) killed himself
- c) became King Solomon's food taster
- d) gave King Solomon all of his money

22.) King Solomon said that Adonijah would not die if Adonijah:
   - a) promised Solomon his concubines
   - b) willed Solomon his estate
   - c) would live in the forest and eat locusts and wild honey
   - d) proved himself worthy

23.) What would happen to Adonijah if he were wicked?

24.) Solomon said to Adonijah:
   - a) I will never forgive you.
   - b) I never want to look upon your countenance again.
   - c) This means war!
   - d) Go to thine house.

25.) Did you know that all of Judah's kings were from the line of David?

? ? ? ? ? ? ? ?

1.) Did you know that God is not mentioned by name in the book of Esther?

2.) The king became angry with Queen Vashti because she:
- a) was ugly
- b) had too many bills on her credit cards
- ✓c) disobeyed him
- d) made more money than he did

3.) Because of his anger with Queen Vashti, the king decreed that:
- a) men with quick tempers should join a twelve-step program
- ✓b) women were to honor men and men were to rule their households
- c) men could have as many as 300 wives
- d) the Equal Rights Amendment should be passed

4.) Why did the king want the people to see Queen Vashti?

5.) Why were all of the fair maidens brought before the king?

6.) Did you know that the name Esther means star?

7.) Mordecai was what relation to Esther?
    ✓a) cousin
    b) financial advisor
    c) mutual fund manager
    d) study partner

8.) Mordecai treated Esther as his daughter because:
    a) she was lovely
    ✓b) she was an orphan
    c) she worked for him
    d) he hoped to get her a part on a television soap opera

9.) The book of Esther was written by:
   a) Moses
   b) Jesus
   c) R.L. Stine
   d) We don't know.

10.) What did the king do when Esther found favor with him?

11.) What had Esther not revealed about herself when she won the contest?

12.) Why didn't Esther reveal her secret?

13.) Mordecai saved the king's life by:
   a) throwing him a life preserver from the sinking ship, *Titanic*
   ✓b) telling him through Esther that his life was in danger from assassins
   c) catching a radio before it landed in his bathwater
   d) warning him about a frayed bungee cord

14.) Mordecai refused to bow to Haman because Mordecai:
✓a) was Jewish
b) had arthritis
c) was a member of a cult that believed in UFOs
d) wanted payment to bow to Haman

15.) What did Haman plan to do to all the Jews?

16.) Did you know that the Jews were bought by Haman for 10,000 silver talents?
If:
I shekel = 64 cents
I mina = 50 shekels
I talent = 60 minas,
then the total price Haman offered for the Jews was: $19,200,000

? ? ? ? ? ? ? ? ?

17.) To replace his sackcloth, Esther sent Mordecai:

    a) a lynx coat

    b) a bearskin rug

    c) designer blue jeans

    d) fine raiment

18.) Why didn't Esther want to speak to the king on her people's behalf?

19.) Esther asked the Jews to do what before she spoke to the king?

    ✓a) fast for three days and nights

    b) sacrifice a ram in her honor

    c) hold another beauty contest

    d) will all of their money to her

20.) When she threw the banquet where she would speak to the king, Esther also invited:

    a) Jesus

    b) Adam

    c) DC Talk

    ✓d) Haman

21.) The king read his records and discovered Mordecai's good deed because the king:

    ✓a) couldn't sleep

    b) was sick in bed with chicken pox

    c) was looking for something to do while waiting for brownies to bake

    d) wanted to read while having his toenails painted

22.) What did the king decide to do for Mordecai for saving his life?

23) After Haman's death, the king gave Mordecai a:

    ✓a) ring

    b) season pass to the nearest amusement park

    c) coupon for a free tattoo

    d) coat of many colors

? ? ? ? ? ? ? ? ?

24.) Whom did Haman think the king wanted to honor?

25.) At the banquet, whom did Esther reveal was the enemy?

26.) To show Esther that her life had been spared, the king:

    a) tapped her on the shoulder with his sword

    b) held a golden scepter toward her

    c) bought her a Newsboys CD

    d) gave her a ring

27.) What holiday was established to remember this event?

28.) Did you know that the Jews still celebrate this holiday?

29.) According to the book of Esther, when should the holiday be observed?

30.) Did you know that the Hebrew month of Adar is February through March on our calendar?

A FAITHFUL SERVANT

Job

1.) Did you know that there are three Wisdom Books in the Bible? They are Job, Proverbs, and Ecclesiastes. Wisdom books deal with human experience through sayings, essays, monologues, or drama.

2.) Where did Job live?
   - a) Uz
   - b) Buzz
   - c) Fuzz
   - d) Scuzz

3.) How many children did Job have?

4.) If God took away Job's possessions, Satan said Job would:
   - a) praise God
   - b) make more money
   - c) start a company called Job's Jobs
   - d) curse God

5.) The Lord told Satan that he must:
   a) give Job back his possessions
   b) raise his children from the dead
   c) turn water into wine
   d) spare Job's life

6.) Satan afflicted Job with painful:
   a) headaches
   b) tax audits from the Internal Revenue Service
   c) sores
   d) bunions

7.) Job's wife advised him to:
   a) will his possessions to her before he died
   b) curse God and die
   c) go on an herbal diet
   d) remain faithful to God

8.) Job was visited by whom during his suffering?

9.) To make peace with Him, what did the Lord command Job's visitors to do?

10.) Job's visitors tried to:
- a) comfort Job
- b) teach him computer skills so he could find a new job
- c) convince him to divorce his wife
- d) run his farm while he was sick

11.) The Lord told Job's visitors that He was:
- a) pleased with them
- b) willing to prosper them
- c) angry that they were unsuccessful at teaching Job new skills
- d) angry about their unfaithfulness to Him

12.) How many years did Job live after his test?

13.) After Job's suffering, God:
- a) gave him twice as much as he had before his suffering
- b) gave him three times as much as he had before his suffering
- c) gave him four times as much as he had before his suffering
- d) allowed Job to win both show-cases on "The Price is Right"

14.) God restored unto Job:
- a) three daughters and seven sons
- b) seven daughters and three sons
- c) ten beautiful daughters
- d) ten handsome sons

15.) Job's new daughters were renowned for their:
- a) wealth
- b) intelligence
- c) victory on "It's Academic"
- d) beauty

BITS OF WISDOM

Proverbs

1.) Solomon was:
- a) a king of Israel
- b) one of the twelve disciples
- c) David's father
- d) a writer for popular TV programs

2.) Who is the giver of wisdom?

3.) A wise person runs away from:
- a) a pesky younger brother
- b) chores
- c) Dad when there's a bad report card
- d) evil

4.) When the Lord loves you, He:
- a) shows you right from wrong
- b) gives you money beyond your dreams
- c) won't let you get chicken pox
- d) will make sure your homework gets done

5.) Happy is the person who finds what?

6.) We should be like ants because they:
- a) work
- b) steal picnic food
- c) are pretty
- d) are quiet

7.) Proverbs lists how many things that the Lord hates?
- a) six
- b) seven
- c) sixty-six
- d) seventeen

8.) Proverbs cautions against:
- a) having too many wives
- b) bad women
- c) letting women talk you into going to a boring party
- d) letting your wife have her way

9.) Did you know that the book of Proverbs was put together in the tenth century before Christ?

10.) You should think of wisdom as your:
- a) mother
- b) daughter
- c) fiancée
- d) sister

11.) Did you know that when the author of Proverbs says to call wisdom your sister, it means that you should hold wisdom in high regard? You can also think of it as walking hand in hand with wisdom, a cherished virtue.

12.) Wisdom is better than:
- a) cherry bubble gum
- b) winning the lottery
- c) rubies
- d) the prizes in happy meals

13.) Who wrote the book of Proverbs?

14.) Did you know that a proverb is a wise saying?

? ? ? ? ? ? ? ? ?

15.) What is the theme of the book of Proverbs?

16.) When you tell a wise person about a mistake, the person will:
    a) laugh at you
    b) love you
    c) hate you
    d) gossip about you

17.) Why does a wise person welcome correction?

18.) According to Proverbs, will wisdom make you live longer?

19.) Hatred stirs anger, but sin is covered by:
    a) hate
    b) anger
    c) love
    d) slime

20.) Does the book of Proverbs advise against gossip?

21.) Why do you think the author of Proverbs would say not to speak badly of others?

22.) A person who will not listen to wise advice will find:
    a) poverty and shame
    b) health and wealth
    c) his own wisdom
    d) a walk-on part on "Saved by the Bell"

23.) A person who heeds wise advice will find:
    a) shame
    b) a winning lottery ticket
    c) honor
    d) fame

24.) What can you do to make someone less angry?

? ? ? ? ? ? ? ?

25.) Pleasant words are like a:
  a) sword
  b) spear
  c) sweet potato pie
  d) honeycomb

26.) What is the crown of an old man?

27.) According to Proverbs, we will be punished if we:
  a) tell lies
  b) beat up the school bully
  c) spend too much time playing computer games
  d) make bad grades in school

28.) Did you know that even a child will be known by his doings? (Proverbs 20:11)

29.) What does Proverbs 20:23 mean by saying a false balance is not good?

30.) Why shouldn't you give good advice to a foolish person?

31.) We shouldn't be jealous of wicked people because they:
- a) will have no reward
- b) will be cursed
- c) know the Lord
- d) will get fat from eating too much rich food

32.) If you are rich, you should:
- a) buy at least three vacation homes
- b) star in a Hollywood movie
- c) eat at the White House with the President
- d) only buy as many things as you need and no more

33.) What would Solomon say about the advertising slogan "Diamonds are forever"?

34.) If your enemy is hungry, you should:
- a) throw a cream pie in his face and laugh
- b) not let him near your parties because he'll eat everything in sight
- c) give him bread to eat
- d) give a donation in his name to the nearest soup kitchen

35.) Did Solomon say it is okay to insult each other as long as it's all in fun?

36.) How would Solomon know about riches?

37.) You will always have enough money if you:
- a) save all of your money
- b) invest in a company called Solomon's Secure Stocks
- c) borrow money from other people but don't pay it back
- d) give to the poor

38.) An angry man:
   - a) is a victim of his surroundings
   - b) should be put on the welfare rolls
   - c) stirs up even more anger
   - d) should be allowed to get away with anything he wants

39.) How many books are in the Old Testament?

40.) Did you know that the Bible has a total of sixty-six books?

THE GOOD WIFE
Proverbs, Chapter 31

1.) A good woman is:
   a) virtuous
   b) beautiful
   c) rich
   d) skinny

2.) What is a virtue?

3.) A good woman is more valuable than what?

4.) Her husband can trust his wife with his:
   a) pet hamster
   b) credit cards
   c) heart
   d) car

5.) What two things does the Proverbs 31 woman seek?

6.) Who gives honor to the good wife?

7.) When it is time to work, she:

    a) passes off her chores to her children

    b) hires the best maid in town

    c) works willingly

    d) calls her mother on the phone and complains

8.) Where does the Proverbs 31 woman get food?

9.) The Proverbs 31 woman starts her day:

    a) before dawn

    b) after she's caught up on all the latest gossip

    c) noon

    d) as soon as her children get in from school

10.) What virtue is described in Proverbs 31:14–19?

11.) The virtue of giving to the poor is called:
   a) flattery
   b) deceit
   c) guile
   d) charity

12.) She is not afraid of snow because:
   a) it gives her a chance to rent videos and eat microwave popcorn all day
   b) she has plenty of clothing to keep her family warm
   c) she has a four-wheel-drive vehicle
   d) the central heating system in her house is always working

13.) What color does the Proverbs 31 woman wear?

14.) Did you know that purple was once worn only by very rich people? In Bible times, purple dye came from a shellfish that could only produce a little color at a time, so the dye was very expensive.

15.) What does the virtuous woman sell?

16.) A good wife wears:
  a) a frown on her face
  b) plenty of red lipstick
  c) only the latest sneakers
  d) strength and honor

17.) When a good woman speaks, what do her words have?

18.) Beauty is not the first concern of the Proverbs 31 woman because she:
  a) already sold her stock in Revlon
  b) is too old to be a model
  c) is not vain or conceited
  d) is vain and conceited

19.) What is more important than beauty in a good woman?

20.) What will happen to the woman who fears the Lord?

? ? ? ? ? ? ? ?

DREAM WEAVER
Daniel

1.) Who wrote the book of Daniel?

2.) Did you know that the book of Daniel is called an apocalypse? Apocalypse means "unveiling". The book of Daniel shows that good will win over evil.

3.) When Daniel had a chance to eat the rich foods of King Nebuchadnezzar, he asked:
   a) for second helpings
   b) a doggy bag
   c) for Pharoah's own steak sauce for his beef wellington
   d) to be excused from eating food forbidden under Jewish dietary laws

4.) When the Lord heard Daniel's request not to eat the king's food, what did the Lord grant Daniel?

5.) What special talent did God give to Daniel that would later help the king?

6.) Did you know that the book of Daniel was written in the Aramaic language?

7.) What did King Nebuchadnezzar say should happen to his wise men when they couldn't interpret his dream?

8.) When King Nebuchadnezzar asked Daniel to interpret his dream, Daniel:
   a) asked the king for more time and prayed to God for wisdom
   b) told the king about the dream right away
   c) asked for more of the king's rich food
   d) presented him with a contract asking for blue M&M candies

9.) King Nebuchadnezzar made an image of what kind of metal?

10.) Did you know that the image King
Nebuchadnezzar made was 90 feet
high? (Daniel 3:1)

11.) Anyone who refused to worship the
image would be:
   a) honored by King
      Nebuchadnezzar
   b) granted the king's daughter's
      hand in marriage
   c) thrown into a fiery furnace
   d) given extra money to buy
      Warheads candy

12.) After the king dreamed of a tree, he:
   a) went to live with the beasts
      of the field, eating grass for
      food
   b) became a forest ranger for the
      U.S. Park Service
   c) walked around the country with
      a pot on his head, planting
      apple seeds
   d) ate wild locusts and honey

13.) Did you know that the king had given Daniel the name Belteshazzar? (Daniel 5:12)

14.) What did King Belshazzar do at his banquet to offend God?

15.) God communicated to King Belshazzar:
    a) with handwriting on a wall
    b) through a burning bush
    c) through the U.S. Post Office
    d) by appearing on TV

16.) Who was the only person who could interpret the handwriting?

17.) Who told King Belshazzar to see Daniel?

18.) Did Daniel's friends worship the image?

? ? ? ? ? ? ? ? ?

19.) What happened when the three Hebrews were thrown into the fiery furnace?

20.) Did you know that many of the dreams and visions recorded in the book of Daniel predict events that still have not taken place?

THE UNWILLING SERVANT
Jonah

1.) Who wrote the book of Jonah?

2.) Did you know that Jonah was the first foreign missionary?

3.) Where did God tell Jonah to go?

4.) Jonah went to:
   a) Ninevah
   b) Tarshish
   c) Joppa
   d) Cleveland

5.) Jonah tried to hide:
   a) on The Love Boat
   b) on a ship heading to Tarshish
   c) at the home of Johnny Quest
   d) under his bed

6.) Did you know that the name "Jonah" means "Dove"?

7.) What did God send out that frightened the people on the ship?

8.) As Jonah slept on the ship, the others called out to:
   a) their gods
   b) Jehovah
   c) a UFO they spotted
   d) a news van from a local TV station

9.) Since he had put them in danger, Jonah told the others to:
   a) be sure they had plenty of food
   b) interpret his dream from the night before
   c) convert to Jonah's faith
   d) throw him overboard

10.) Did they throw Jonah overboard right away?

11.) Did you know that the Bible does not say that Jonah was swallowed by a whale, but a great fish? (Jonah 1:17)

12.) After Jonah was thrown overboard, the sea:

    a) grew even rougher

    b) made big waves for the surf dudes to ride

    c) parted

    d) grew calm

13.) What did Jonah do while he was inside the fish?

14.) After the fish vomited Jonah onto dry land, the Lord told Jonah to:

    a) take a bath

    b) go to Ninevah

    c) return home

    d) apologize to the men on the ship

15.) Did you know that the city of Ninevah was so large that it took three days to walk all the way around it? (Jonah 3:3)

? ? ? ? ? ? ? ?

16.) How long was Jonah inside the fish?

17.) What was Jonah's message to Ninevah from God?

18.) Upon hearing the message, the people of Ninevah:
   a) fasted and wore sackcloth
   b) ate a big turkey dinner and put on Pilgrim costumes
   c) ate only chocolate and wore only purple for three days
   d) celebrated Lent

19.) When the king of Ninevah heard the message, he sat in:
   a) his throne
   b) the third row seat of the movie theater
   c) ashes
   d) the city dump

20.) What happened when God saw that the citizens of Ninevah had repented?

21.) Did you know that the repentance of Ninevah is the biggest revival known to man?

22.) When the city repented, Jonah:
    a) rejoiced
    b) was angry
    c) threw a big party
    d) was the guest of honor at a big banquet given by the king

23.) Did you know that Jonah 4:2 gives us clues about God's character? In this verse, Jonah describes God as gracious, merciful, slow to anger, and kind.

24.) Why did Jonah want to stay near Ninevah?

25.) For shelter, God gave Jonah a:
    a) beautiful mansion
    b) sunflower
    c) mobile home
    d) gourd

26.) How did Jonah feel after God took away his shelter?

27.) By killing the plant Jonah loved, what lesson did God teach Jonah?

28.) Did you know about 120,000 people lived in Ninevah? (Jonah 4:11)

29.) The Bible has:
   a) six books
   b) sixteen books
   c) sixty-six books
   d) six hundred books

30.) Did you know that there are thirty-nine books in the Old Testament?

MATTHEW'S GOSPEL
Matthew

1.) Who wrote the book of Matthew?

2.) Did you know that Matthew was a tax collector?

3.) The book of Matthew starts by recording:
    a) Jesus' birth
    b) the creation
    c) St. Paul's birth
    d) Jesus' birth line, or genealogy

4.) Did you know that it was unusual for birth records to mention women, although Matthew mentions them in his gospel?

5.) In what city was Jesus born?

6.) Did you know that the King Herod of Jesus' time was known as Herod the Great?

7.) King Herod sought the baby Jesus to:
    a) worship Him
    b) give Him gold, frankincense, and myrrh
    c) give Mary and Joseph money for a hotel room at Embassy Suites
    d) kill Jesus

8.) To keep Him safe from Herod, Mary and Joseph took Jesus to:
    a) Egypt
    b) Uz
    c) Edom
    d) Paris

9.) The food John the Baptist ate was:
    a) manna
    b) cookies made by elves
    c) milk and honey
    d) locusts and wild honey

10.) Did you know that all of the Gospels record the ministry of John the Baptist?

11.) How long was Jesus tempted by the devil?

12.) What would Peter and Andrew fish for if they followed Jesus?

13.) Another name for Jesus' Sermon on the Mount is:
   a) Beatitudes
   b) Attitude Adjustments
   c) Beatniks
   d) Assertiveness Training

14.) Did you know that the comparisons of Christians to salt and light are called Similitudes?

15.) What do we call the prayer Jesus taught His disciples?

16.) Jesus said to store your treasures in:
   a) the stock market
   b) mutual funds
   c) real estate
   d) heaven

? ? ? ? ? ? ? ? ?

17.) Did you know that in New Testament times, a worker earned about sixteen cents a day?

18.) What do we call Jesus' command to do unto others as you would have them to unto you?

19.) The relative of Peter's whom Jesus healed was Peter's:
   a) second cousin twice removed
   b) kissin' cousin
   c) step-great-grandmother
   d) mother-in-law

20.) What is another name for the stories Jesus used to teach people?

21.) How many disciples did Jesus call?

22.) When the disciples saw Jesus walking on the water, they thought He was a:
   a) ghost
   b) hologram
   c) hallucination
   d) mirage

23.) Jesus healed the Canaanite woman's daughter because of her:
    a) great faith
    b) gift of gold, frankincense, and myrrh
    c) desire to wash His feet with perfume
    d) gift of a video game set and several cartridges

24.) Did Jesus know He was to be crucified?

25.) We should be watchful because:
    a) someone might steal our treasures
    b) we don't know when the Lord will return
    c) we might have forgotten to turn on our security systems
    d) our watchdog is at the vet

26.) Which disciple agreed to betray Jesus?

? ? ? ? ? ? ? ? ?

27.) Jesus was betrayed in exchange for:
   a) nothing
   b) tickets to a concert
   c) the widow's mite
   d) thirty pieces of silver

28.) What was the name of the garden where Jesus prayed before His crucifixion?

29.) When Jesus asked His disciples to watch with Him as He prayed, they:
   a) slept
   b) obeyed
   c) ate the leftover bread and fish from the lunch Jesus fed the 5000
   d) played Uno

30.) Judas betrayed Jesus with the following sign:
   a) cutting off His right ear with a sword
   b) kissing Him
   c) denying Him three times
   d) offering Him a meal of locusts and wild honey

31.) After Judas betrayed Jesus, he:
   a) repented
   b) spent his money on video rentals
   c) went into the Federal Witness Protection Program
   d) was interviewed on the news program "20/20"

32.) Did you know that Judas's betrayal of Jesus is told in all of the Gospels?

33.) What did the centurion say when the earth quaked at Jesus' crucifixion?

34.) The stone on the door of Jesus' tomb was rolled back by:
   a) Judas
   b) Mary Magdalene
   c) Pharoah
   d) an angel

? ? ? ? ? ? ? ? ?

35.) The risen Jesus said He would meet His disciples at:

    a) Galilee
    b) His mother's house for pizza
    c) Smokey Joe's Cafe
    d) the Bethlehem Drive-in theater

36.) Where did Jesus tell Peter to get money for taxes?

37.) Did you know that the penny (denarius) Jesus mentions in Matthew 20:2 was the most common coin at that time?

38.) Why didn't the soldiers on watch at the tomb admit that the Son of God had risen?

39.) What does Jesus' resurrection prove?

40.) What is the last word in the book of Matthew?

JOHN'S JOURNEY WITH JESUS
John

1.) Who wrote the book of John?

2.) Did you know that the book of John does not record the events surrounding Jesus' birth?

3.) Where did Jesus perform His first miracle?
  a) Cane
  b) Cain
  c) Cana
  d) Cathy

4.) Who told Jesus there was no more wine?

5.) The event where Jesus performed His first miracle was a:
  a) circus
  b) bar mitzvah
  c) wedding
  d) birthday party

6.) Did you know that the author of the Book of John was one of Jesus' twelve disciples?

7.) When Jesus saw the moneychangers at the temple, He:
   a) bought three doves and two goats
   b) asked for change for the vending machines
   c) asked what time the Bible study on the book of Revelation would occur
   d) overturned their tables and angrily rebuked them

8.) God promises believers:
   a) earthly riches
   b) eternal life
   c) manna
   d) a year's supply of Rice a Roni, the San Francisco treat

9.) What did Jesus ask the woman at the well to give Him?

10.) What important news did Jesus tell the woman about Himself?

11.) Jesus fed a large crowd of people with:
   a) five barley loaves and two small fish
   b) three cans of soda and a pack of M&Ms
   c) five candy bars and a pint of lemonade
   d) five coffee beans and a peanut butter and jelly sandwich

12.) How many people were in the crowd?

13.) Jesus was betrayed by:
   a) Judas Iscariot
   b) Moses
   c) Pharoah
   d) James Bond, Agent 007

14.) What did Jesus do to serve His disciples at the Last Supper?

15.) What lesson did this teach the disciples?

16.) Did you know that Jesus showed
He knew who would betray Him by
giving Judas bread dipped in wine?

17.) Did Jesus know that Peter would deny
Him three times?

18.) Immediately after Peter had denied
Jesus three times, a:
   a) donkey brayed
   b) fire engine siren went off
   c) rooster crowed
   d) woman screamed

19.) Did you know that all four gospels tell
us about Peter's denial of Jesus?

20.) When Pilate presented Jesus to the
mob during Passover, they cried:
   a) He is our king!
   b) Have mercy on Him!
   c) For He's a jolly good fellow!
   d) Crucify Him!

21.) What will we do if we love Jesus?

22.) What did the sign Pilate made for Jesus' cross say?

23.) Did you know that Pilate's sign was written in Hebrew, Greek, and Latin? (John 19:20)

24.) What did Jesus say as He died on the cross?

25.) The angels at Jesus' tomb said to Mary Magdalene:
   a) Why weepest thou?
   b) Fetch us something to eat.
   c) We know you have been married five times.
   d) Why are there so many women named Mary in the Bible?

26.) What did the risen Jesus say to Mary Magdalene?

27.) Did Thomas believe the disciples when they said they had seen the risen Christ?

28.) The fact that Jesus rose from the dead proves that Jesus is:
   a) a good teacher
   b) a religious leader
   c) really, really smart
   d) the Son of God, who is worthy to be worshiped

29.) John says he wrote his book so you will:
   a) feed the poor
   b) be healthy, wealthy, and wise
   c) be a good person
   d) believe in Jesus Christ, the Son of God, and have life in His name

30.) What is the last word in the book of John?

NEWS FOR THE ROMANS

Paul's Epistle to the Romans

1.) Who wrote the Epistle to the Romans?

2.) The letter was written to:
   a) Roman Christians
   b) Caesar
   c) the owner of Roma Restaurant
   d) the Vatican Council

3.) Did you know that the letter to the Romans was written almost sixty years after Jesus was crucified?

4.) The letter is written about:
   a) Roman Christians
   b) the Vatican Council
   c) why they should give Paul money for his mission work
   d) Jesus Christ our Lord, the Son of God

5.) What proof does Paul offer that Jesus is holy?

6.) Did you know that the term "saint" applies to any Christian? Paul tells the Roman Christians that they are called to be saints. (Romans 1:7)

7.) We can have peace with God through:
    a) random acts of kindness
    b) helping an old lady cross the street every day
    c) making sure we give 10% of our allowance to church every Sunday
    d) faith in our Lord Jesus Christ

8.) To receive salvation, we have to pay Jesus:
    a) by being ministers and missionaries when we grow up whether we want to or not
    b) by spending at least an hour a day reading the Bible
    c) by ignoring people who tease us
    d) nothing. His gift of salvation is free.

9.) Who makes us righteous?

10.) Did you know that the old man Paul talks about is our old nature that wants to sin? (Romans 6:6)

11.) Christians live under grace instead of having to follow laws. This is called:
   a) the New Covenant
   b) the Declaration of Independence
   c) the Apostles' Creed
   d) the Girl Scout Pledge

12.) Once you stop living for sin, you are guided by:
   a) your minister
   b) your Sunday School teacher
   c) your friends
   d) the Holy Spirit

13.) What two things will you find if you live in the Spirit?

14.) Is any person righteous without Jesus?

15.) When a Christian is too sad or upset to pray, what does the Holy Spirit do?

16.) When we pray, whose plan shall be carried out?
  a) ours
  b) God's
  c) our pastor's
  d) our parents'

17.) We can be separated from God's love by:
  a) not going to church every Wednesday and Sunday
  b) bad people
  c) too much television
  d) nothing

18.) What does Paul mean when he writes: "Even us, whom he hath called, not of the Jews only, but also of the Gentiles"?

19.) Did you know that the Gentiles were the unbelievers of Bible times?

20.) Which one of the twelve tribes of Israel was Paul from?

21.) Paul said he was Jewish so the Roman Christians would know that:
    a) God has not forgotten His chosen people
    b) Paul was better than the Roman Christians
    c) Paul had paid handsomely to have a professional trace his family line
    d) Paul was eligible to be a member of Boy Scouts

22.) The Romans were:
    a) Jewish
    b) Catholic
    c) Gentiles
    d) popular

23.) Paul wrote that he was an apostle of whom?

? ? ? ? ? ? ? ?

24.) Did you know that in this letter Paul gives us a clue as to God's character? He describes God as possessing matchless knowledge and wisdom. (Romans 11:33)

25.) As to our gifts from God, Paul said:
   a) all Christians have equal gifts
   b) we should go to classes to develop our gifts
   c) that for a small fee, he would help the Romans find their gifts
   d) we should use whatever gifts God gave us

26.) Who is in charge of seeking revenge for evil?

27.) Evil will be overcome by:
   a) evil
   b) cutting others down
   c) the sword
   d) good

28.) Who will judge all of us?

29.) What is the last word in this letter?

THE THESSALONIANS
I and II Thessalonians

1.) Who wrote the epistles to the Thessalonians?

2.) The name of the place where the Thessalonians lived was:
   a) Thesis
   b) Thessalonica
   c) Toronto
   d) Thessa

3.) Did you know that the epistles to the Thessalonians were written in A.D. 51?

4.) The group of Thessalonians Paul was writing to was the:
   a) church
   b) people who would finance his retirement
   c) pagans
   d) Gentiles

5.) Did you know that an epistle is a letter?

6.) After greeting the Thessalonians, Paul:
- a) praises them
- b) asks for a love offering
- c) tells them to start a Bible college
- d) tells them not to buy a Cadillac when a Ford would serve their purpose

7.) Paul tells them that when they talk they should:
- a) not offend anyone
- b) be sure they are recorded on videotape
- c) not forget to ask for money
- d) worry about pleasing God, not people

8.) Whom did Paul say tried to keep him from making progress?

9.) Did you know that the word edify means to teach, educate, or guide spiritually? Paul says that Christians should edify each other. (I Thessalonians 5:11)

10.) Paul tells the Thessalonians to:
   a) love one another
   b) take turns with the household chores
   c) carry swords at all times
   d) vote Republican

11.) Paul says that Christians should put on:
   a) cosmetics that have not been tested on animals
   b) a happy face
   c) the breastplate of faith and love and a helmet of hope and salvation
   d) army uniforms

12.) What else did Paul tell us to do in I Thessalonians 5:11?

13.) What did Paul say to do without ceasing?

? ? ? ? ? ? ? ? ?

14.) Paul said never to seem:
- a) evil
- b) too friendly to the pagans
- c) unwilling to share
- d) uncool

15.) The last word in the first letter to the Thessalonians is:
- a) hello
- b) g'day
- c) Godspeed
- d) Amen.

? ? ? ? ? ? ? ?

HEBREWS

1.) Who wrote The Epistle to the Hebrews?

2.) Did you know that twenty-one books of the New Testament are epistles?

3.) An epistle is a:
   a) letter
   b) book
   c) novel
   d) wife of an apostle

4.) Today, God speaks to us:
   a) through a megaphone
   b) by playing recordings backwards
   c) by appearing in a burning bush
   d) through His Son Jesus

5.) Whom does the author of Hebrews trust?

6.) As the perfect Son of God, what does Jesus offer to all who obey Him?

7.) What are angels?

8.) If we accept Jesus, we will find:
  a) a way to make good grades in school
  b) mercy and grace
  c) a lot of money
  d) many friends

9.) Good deeds are not as important to the Christian as:
  a) faith
  b) voting
  c) having more video games than anyone else
  d) being the most popular person in school

10.) What does God think of good works done in His name?

11.) Did you know that today Christians live under the new covenant described in Hebrews? The old Mosaic covenant meant that God's people followed a set of rules. Under the new covenant,

Jesus died for our sins. We are forgiven if we accept Jesus as our personal savior. (Hebrews 8:12–13)

12.) To please God, a Christian must have:
   a) given up chocolate for Lent
   b) gone to Vacation Bible School every year for five years
   c) a wardrobe of Christian T-shirts and at least 10 CDs by Christian musicians
   d) faith

13.) Name at least two people of faith described in Hebrews.

14.) Where is Jesus now?

15.) What is the last word of the letter to the Hebrews?

16.) Instead of burnt offerings, what sacrifice should we offer to God?

? ? ? ? ? ? ? ?

17.) God corrects us because He:
   a) will benefit
   b) wants all Christians to be missionaries to the North Pole
   c) wants us to learn how to be holy
   d) thinks it is fun

18.) No one will see God without:
   a) a certificate of baptism
   b) permission from St. Peter at the pearly gates
   c) teaching Sunday School for twenty years
   d) holiness

19.) Some have entertained strangers who were really:
   a) angels
   b) St. Paul
   c) St. Peter at the pearly gates
   d) members of Michael W. Smith's band

20.) Why should we ignore strange teachings?

JOHN'S LETTERS

I, II, and III John

1.) What is an epistle?

2.) How many epistles did John write?

3.) The Epistles of John were written by:
   a) John the Baptist
   b) Jonathan Pierce
   c) Jonathan Taylor Thomas
   d) John the Apostle

4.) If we say we have no sin, we are fooling:
   a) ourselves
   b) our parents
   c) our teachers
   d) our friends

5.) Did you know that when John writes about little children, he means all Christians?

6.) What commandment does John repeat?

7.) To show us His love, God:
- a) sent His only begotten Son into the world, that we might live through Him
- b) sent manna to all Christians
- c) promised vast wealth to all Christians
- d) promised that one day we would have pictures of Mars

8.) Throughout his first letter, John tells Christians not to love:
- a) their brothers
- b) pagans
- c) television
- d) the world

9.) John says that true Christians have:
- a) love
- b) fear
- c) gold plaques with their names engraved on them
- d) money invested in John's real estate firm

10.) How does John define God?

11.) What will happen to those who say that Jesus is the Son of God?

12.) Whom will you love if you also love God?

13.) Did you know that I John 5:7 was probably not written by John, but added later?

14.) John tells the little children to stay away from:
   a) bad movies
   b) cereal with too much sugar
   c) violent video games
   d) idols

15.) What is the last word in John's first letter?

16.) Did you know that the elect lady John speaks of in his second letter is probably another name for a church?

17.) What three blessings does John wish his readers?

18.) John says that when someone pretends to be a Christian but really isn't, you should:
- a) not let the person into your house
- b) pretend you don't speak English
- c) spread the blood of a lamb on your door
- d) tell everybody at school

19.) Why does John say you should not wish a false Christian well?

20.) Why is John's second letter short?

21.) The final word in John's second epistle is:
- a) Adios
- b) Bonjour
- c) Cheerio
- d) Amen

22.) Did you know that John's third letter is written to his friend Gaius?

23.) What blessings did John wish Gaius?

24.) Gaius was:

    a) a strong Christian who walked in the truth

    b) a pagan John was trying to convert

    c) one of the twelve disciples

    d) a rich merchant who gave John millions of dollars to run his ministry

25) John was angry with Diotrephes because Diotrephes:

    a) was more concerned about his reputation than he was about other Christians

    b) refused to let John marry his daughter

    c) did not offer John snails cooked in garlic sauce for dinner

    d) made corrections to John's second epistle with red ink

26.) Who has not seen God?

27.) He that does _____ is of God.

28.) John said Demetrius was godly because he:
- a) did not like Diotrephes
- b) praised all of John's epistles
- c) was a true Christian witness
- d) gave John fine food and lodgings

29.) John's third epistle is short because he:
- a) was running late because he wasted too much time on computer games
- b) ran out of things to write
- c) ran out of ink
- d) hoped to see them in person soon

30.) What does John wish Gaius in the letter's closing?

A WORD FROM JUDE

Jude

1.) Who wrote the Epistle of Jude?

2.) Did you know that Jude was one of Jesus' brothers?

3.) This letter is written to:
   - a) Christians in the early church
   - b) Paul the Apostle
   - c) Jesus
   - d) Elvis Presley

4.) What three things does Jude wish for his readers?

5.) Jude was upset with ungodly men in the church because they:
   - a) did not give their full 10% tithe
   - b) denied our Lord God and His Son Jesus Christ
   - c) sacrificed bulls instead of bullocks
   - d) spent all of the church's money on themselves

6.) Jude told his readers to remember two cities that were punished by God. What are the names of the cities?

7.) Jude warns his readers not to be like:
   a) Abel
   b) Cain
   c) Hollywood stars
   d) Moses

8.) Jude says that people who don't love the Lord:
   a) are nice people if you can forget about their unbelief
   b) never loan you any paper if you forget to bring yours to school
   c) copy off of your paper during tests
   d) will say nice things they don't mean to important people who can help them

9.) Name another book of the Bible whose wise sayings warn about flatterers.

10.) What is the last word of Jude's epistle?

11.) People who deny Jesus Christ:
    a) are more interested in worldly things like being rich and popular than in God
    b) will always be famous because they shock people
    c) are true Christians
    d) will go to heaven

12.) How can Christians build themselves up?

13.) Christians should keep themselves:
    a) in church at all times
    b) on every church committee to show God how hard they work
    c) in with the bad crowd at school
    d) in God's love

14.) What does Jesus Christ offer us?

15.) To whom does Jude give praise and glory?

ANSWERS

1.) **Moses**

2.) **(Genesis 1:3–5) He separated day and night.**

3.) **(Genesis 1:14-19) the sun, the moon, and the stars**

5.) **(Genesis 2:10) to water the garden**

6.) **(Genesis 2:19) d) Adam**

7.) **(Genesis 2:19) Adam**

8.) **(Genesis 2:18) as a helpmate for Adam**

9.) **(Genesis 3:20) c) Eve**

11.) (Genesis 2:21) a rib

13.) (Genesis 3:1) a) serpent

14.) (Genesis 3:5) d) knowledge of good and evil

16.) (Genesis 3:7) They sewed themselves aprons made of fig leaves.

17.) (Genesis 3:8) They hid themselves.

18.) (Genesis 3:12) d) Eve

19.) (Genesis 3:22–24) a) sent them out of Eden

20.) (Genesis 3:24) cherubim

? ? ? ? ? ? ? ? ?

FIRST MURDER/THE FLOOD

1.) (Genesis 4:1) Cain

2.) (Genesis 4:2) Abel

4.) (Genesis 4:16) b) Nod

6.) (Genesis 4:25) Seth

7.) (Genesis 5:22) Enoch

8.) (Genesis 5:22, 24) that he walked with God.

9.) (Genesis 5:27) d) 969

10.) (Genesis 6:14) c) an ark

12.) (Genesis 7:6) 600 years old

13.) (Genesis 10:1) a) Ham

15.) the Pentateuch

1.) (Genesis 11:4) c) the Tower of Babel

2.) (Genesis 11:7–8) He caused them to speak different languages and scattered them over the earth.

4.) (Genesis 13:10) the plain of Jordan

6.) (Genesis 16:15) a) the mother of Ishmael

7.) (Genesis 16:16) c) 86

8.) (Genesis 17:5) b) Abraham

9.) Because He had promised to make him the father of many nations.

12.) Moses

13.) (Genesis 17:17) d) laughed

14.) (Genesis 17:17) because Sarai was very old

15.) (Genesis 19:28) a) Sodom and Gomorrah

16.) (Genesis 19:26) She turned into a pillar of salt.

17.) d) Her name is not recorded in the Bible.

19.) (Genesis 24:3) a) Canaanites

20.) (Genesis 24:22) d) gold jewelry

21.) (Genesis 31:41) 14 years

22.) (Genesis 37:3) Israel

23.) (Genesis 37:3) a) was the child of his old age

24.) (Genesis 37:3) a coat of many colors

25.) (Genesis 37:6–8) b) his brothers would serve Joseph

26.) (Genesis 41:48) stored food for the future

27.) (Genesis 50:26) a) Joseph's death

? ? ? ? ? ? ? ?

ONE BIG EXIT

1.) **Moses**

3.) (Exodus 1:11) b) slaves

4.) (Exodus 1:11) d) treasure cities

5.) (Exodus 2:5–6) Pharoah's daughter

6.) (Exodus 2:5) at the river, getting ready to take a bath

8.) (Exodus 3:2) c) burning bush

9.) (Exodus 3:8) b) a land flowing with milk and honey

10.) (Exodus 4:3) a serpent

11.) (Exodus 7:20) a) blood

13.) (Exodus 11:2) d) silver and gold

14.) (Exodus 12:27) Passover

15.) (Exodus 14:13-31) the parting of the Red Sea

16.) d) Moses

17.) (Exodus 16:5) No. They were to gather twice their daily allotment on the day before the Sabbath.

18.) (Exodus 16:12) because the Israelites complained

19.) (Exodus 16:13) c) quail

20.) (Exodus 20) b) the Ten Commandments

21.) (Exodus 28:1) a) Aaron

22.) (Exodus 32:4) b) a golden calf

23.) d) Pentateuch

24.) (Exodus 16:31) manna

25.) (Exodus 37:8–9) cherubs and cherubim

1.) In The book of Judges.

2.) Judges ruled Israel.

4.) (Judges 13:4 and 7) d) wine or strong drink

5.) (Judges 13:11–16) a) Samson's father Manoah

6.) (Judges 13:18) It was a secret.

7.) (Judges 14:3) d) Philistine

8.) (Judges 14:5–6) a) killed it with his bare hands

9.) (Judges 14:8) c) a swarm of bees and honey

10.) (Judges 14:13) He challenged them to solve a riddle.

11.) (Judges 14:17) b) Samson's wife

12.) (Judges 14:20) a) Samson's friend

14.) (Judges 15:16) d) donkey's jawbone

15.) (Judges 14:19) He went to the next Philistine town, slew 30 men, and took their cloaks.

16.) (Judges 15:19) d) the donkey's jawbone

17.) (Judges 16:5) a) 1100 pieces of silver each

20.) (Judges 16:7) c) were tied with seven green cords of rope

21.) (Judges 16:11) c) new rope that had never been used

22.) (Judges 16:13) He told her that his hair had to be woven in seven strands into the web of a loom.

23.) (Judges 16) He broke free easily.

24.) (Judges 16:16) b) pestered Samson every day to tell her until he confessed

25.) (Judges 16:22) It began to grow again.

27.) b) was no longer walking with the Lord

28.) (Judges 16:23–24) because Samson had been captured

29.) (Judges 16:27) 3000

30.) (Judges 16:28–30) b) prayed to God for strength

31.) (Judges 16:30) He killed everyone at the gathering. In death, Samson killed more Philistines than he had at any time in his life.

? ? ? ? ? ? ? ? ?

1.) No

3.) (Ruth 1:1) d) There wasn't enough food to eat because of famine.

4.) (Ruth 1:2) a) Moab

5.) (Ruth 1:1) Bethlehem-judah

6.) (Ruth 1:14) Ruth

7.) (Ruth 1:4) b) Orpah and Ruth

8.) (Ruth 1:4–5) ten years

9.) (Ruth 1:7) d) return to her homeland

10.) (Ruth 1:8) a) go back and live with their mothers

11.) (Ruth 1:3) He died.

13.) (Ruth 1:16) d) convert to Judaism

14.) (Ruth 1:20) a) changed her name to Mara

15.) (Ruth 1:22) barley

16.) (Ruth 2:2) gleaned the fields

18.) (Ruth 2:3) a) Naomi's husband

19.) (Ruth 2:9) a) that she would be safe and have plenty of water to drink

20.) (Ruth 2:10–11) d) had taken good care of Naomi

21.) (Ruth 2:23) barley and wheat

22.) No.

23.) (Ruth 3:1–4) a) ask Boaz what to do next

24.) (Ruth 3:17) a) six measures of barley

? ? ? ? ? ? ?

25.) (Ruth 4:9) the property that had belonged to Naomi's sons and husband

26.) (Ruth 4:5–6) b) Ruth was a Moabite

27.) (Ruth 4:11) a) accept Ruth as one of their own

28.) (Ruth 4:13) c) married Ruth

30.) sixty-six

? ? ? ? ? ? ? ?

2.) (I Samuel 1:8) a) she had no children

3.) (I Samuel 1:11) She asked to give birth to a son.

4.) (I Samuel 1:11) b) that her son would belong to God

5.) (I Samuel 1:11) d) cut

6.) (I Samuel 1:20) Hannah gave birth to a son.

8.) (I Samuel 1:25) a) Eli the priest

10.) (I Samuel 1:28) She wanted him to serve the Lord all of his life.

11.) (I Samuel 2:12) c) evil

12.) (I Samuel 2:18) a) ministered before the Lord

13.) (I Samuel 2:19) c) little coat

14.) (I Samuel 2:20) a) blessed Hannah and her husband Elkanah

15.) (I Samuel 3:8–10) Samuel answered the Lord on the fourth call.

16.) (I Samuel 2:21) yes

18.) (I Samuel 2:34) The Lord said that both of them would die.

19.) (I Samuel 3:3) a) evil

20.) (I Samuel 2:35) d) raise up His own priest who would do His will

21.) (I Samuel 3:5) a) Eli

22.) (I Samuel 3:2) a) sleeping

23.) (I Samuel 3:11–14) d) punish Eli's house because Eli's sons were evil

24.) (I Samuel 3:20) b) prophet

FROM JUDGES TO A KING

2.) (I Samuel 8:1) b) made his sons judges in his place

3.) (I Samuel 8:3) a) took bribes and did not rule fairly

4.) (I Samuel 8:2) Joel and Abiah.

5.) (I Samuel 8:3) yes

7.) (I Samuel 8:6) b) prayed to the Lord

8.) (I Samuel 8:9) a) let the people see how a king would rule

9.) (I Samuel 8:7) the Lord Himself

10.) (I Samuel 8:10–17) a) greedy

11.) (I Samuel 8:19) No. They still wanted a king.

12.) Saul

14.) (I Samuel 9:2) d) being the tallest and most handsome man in all of Israel

15.) (I Samuel 9:3) a) his father's lost donkeys

17.) (I Samuel 9:15–17) b) God had told Samuel in his ear that Saul was the one.

18.) (I Samuel 9:21) d) was from the smallest of the twelve tribes of Israel and his family was not important

19.) (I Samuel 9:20) Samuel told Saul that the donkeys had been found.

20.) (I Samuel 10:1) Samuel anointed Saul king.

21.) (I Samuel 9:11) young women drawing water from the well

23.) (I Samuel 10:10) b) prophecy

24.) (I Samuel 10:16) No. The anointing had taken place privately.

1.) (I Samuel 15:23) because Saul disobeyed God

3.) (I Samuel 16:6) a) handsome

4.) (I Samuel 16:7) d) hearts

5.) (I Samuel 16:1) Jesse

6.) (I Samuel 16:10) seven

7.) (I Samuel 16:12) b) glowing with health and handsome to look at

8.) (I Samuel 16:12) The Lord told Samuel to anoint David king.

9.) (I Samuel 16:15–17) Because God had sent an evil spirit to bother rebellious Saul

10.) (I Samuel 16:16) d) harp

11.) (I Samuel 16:12) David

13.) (I Samuel 16:21) a) loved Saul and became his armor-bearer

14.) (I Samuel 17:4) a Philistine giant from Gath who taunted the Israelites

16.) (I Samuel 17:13) the three eldest brothers, Eliab, Abinadab, and Shammah

17.) (I Samuel 17:15) d) fed his father's sheep in Bethlehem

18.) (I Samuel 17:16) forty

19.) (I Samuel 17:17–18) a) take them food

20.) (I Samuel 17:23) d) Goliath's challenge to the army

21.) (I Samuel 17:25) c) riches, Saul's daughter, and freedom

22.) (I Samuel 17:32) c) fight Goliath

23.) (I Samuel 17:34–36) c) killed a lion and a bear who tried to steal his father's sheep

24.) (I Samuel 17:37) David had faith that the Lord would keep him safe.

25.) (I Samuel 17:40) five

26.) (I Samuel 17:42–43) b) made fun of David

27.) (I Samuel 17:46) c) everyone would know about God

29.) (I Samuel 17:51) They ran away.

30.) (I Samuel 17:28) He was angry. Eliab accused David of being naughty and only wanting to see the excitement. Eliab also feared that David had left the family's sheep untended.

? ? ? ? ? ? ? ?

THE KINGS RULE

2.) (I Kings 1:1) He is old and ill.

3.) (I Kings 1:5) c) Solomon's older half-brother

4.) (I Kings 1:5) a) he would be the next king

6.) (I Kings 1:6) no

7.) (I Kings 1:6) a) handsome

8.) (I Kings 1:11) Bathsheba

9.) (I Kings 1:13) a) speak to King David about Adonijah

10.) (I Kings 1:13) d) Solomon was supposed to be the next king, not Adonijah

11.) (I Kings 1:18) no

12.) (I Kings 1:10) Solomon

14.) (I Kings 1:33–34) a) had Solomon anointed and declared king

15.) (I Kings 1:38) King David's own mule.

16.) (I Kings 1:39) a) trumpet

17.) (I Kings 1:43) Jonathan

18.) (I Kings 1:47) b) King David

19.) (I Kings 1:48) He had seen the events with his own eyes.

20.) (I Kings 1:49) d) rose up and left the party in fear

21.) (I Kings 1:51) a) begged King Solomon not to kill him

22.) (I Kings 1:52) d) proved himself worthy

23.) (I Kings 1:52) Adonijah would die.

24.) (I Kings 1:53) d) Go to thine house.

2.) (Esther 1:12) c) disobeyed him

3.) (Esther 1:20–22) b) women were to honor men and men were to rule their households

4.) (Esther 1:11) because of her great beauty

5.) (Esther 2:4) so he could find a new queen

7.) (Esther 2:7) a) cousin

8.) (Esther 2:7) b) she was an orphan

9.) d) We don't know

10.) (Esther 2:17) crowned her the new queen

11.) (Esther 2:10) that she was Jewish

12.) (Esther 2:10) because Mordecai told her not to

13.) (Esther 2:21–22) b) telling him through Esther that his life was in danger from assassins

14.) (Esther 3:4) a) was Jewish

15.) (Esther 3:9) destroy them

17.) (Esther 4:4) d) fine raiment

18.) (Esther 4:11) The king had not summoned her, so asking to speak to him was risking her life.

19.) (Esther 4:16) a) fast for three days and nights

20.) (Esther 5:12) d) Haman

21.) (Esther 6:1) a) couldn't sleep

22.) (Esther 6:3) honor Mordecai

23.) (Esther 8:2) a) ring

24.) (Esther 6:6) Haman

25.) (Esther 7:6) Haman

26.) (Esther 8:4) b) held a golden scepter toward her

27.) (Esther 9:19,26) the Feast of Purim

29.) (Esther 9:21) The fourteenth and fifteenth days of Adar

? ? ? ? ? ? ? ? ?

A FAITHFUL SERVANT

2.) (Job 1:1) a) Uz

3.) (Job 1:2) ten; seven sons and three
daughters

4.) (Job 1:11) d) curse God

5.) (Job 2:6) d) spare Job's life

6.) (Job 2:7) c) sores

7.) (Job 2:9) b) curse God and die

8.) (Job 2:11) three friends

9.) (Job 42:8) To make a burnt offering
of seven bulls and seven rams

10. (Job 2:11) a) comfort Job

11.) (Job 42:7) d) angry about their
unfaithfulness to Him

12.) (Job 42:16) 140

13.) (Job 42:10) a) gave him twice as much as he had before his suffering

14.) (Job 42:12) a) three daughters and seven sons

15.) (Job 42:15) d) beauty

? ? ? ? ? ? ? ?

BITS OF WISDOM

1.) (Proverbs 1:1) a) a king of Israel

2.) (Proverbs 2:6) the Lord

3.) (Proverbs 3:7) d) evil

4.) (Proverbs 3:12) a) shows you right from wrong

5.) (Proverbs 3:13) wisdom

6.) (Proverbs 6:6–8) a) work

7.) (Proverbs 6:16) b) seven

8.) (Proverbs 6:24) b) bad women

10.) (Proverbs 7:4) d) sister

12.) (Proverbs 8:11) c) rubies

13.) Solomon wrote most of it, although some portions are attributed to others.

15.) Wisdom

16.) (Proverbs 9:8) b) love you

17.) Because the wise person is always trying to be wiser. Learning from others is
a way to do that.

18.) (Proverbs 9:11) yes

19.) (Proverbs 10:12) c) love

20.) (Proverbs 11:13) yes

21.) Speaking badly of others is hurtful, and
gossip is not always true. Have you
ever been hurt by something someone
said about you?

22.) (Proverbs 13:18) a) poverty and shame
23.) (Proverbs 13:18) c) honor

24.) (Proverbs 15:1) Give the person a kind
answer.

25.) (Proverbs 16:24) d) honeycomb

26.) (Proverbs 17:6) his grandchildren

27.) (Proverbs 19:5) a) tell lies

29.) It means that God does not want people to cheat each other. For instance, God would not want a butcher to charge you for two pounds of meat when he is only selling you one.

30.) (Proverbs 23:9) because a foolish person does not appreciate good advice

31.) (Proverbs 24:19–20) a) will have no reward

32.) (Proverbs 25:16) d) only buy as many things as you need and no more

33.) (Proverbs 27:24) He would say that riches are not forever.

? ? ? ? ? ? ? ? ?

34.) (Proverbs 25:21) c) give him bread to eat

35.) (Proverbs 26:19) no

36.) King Solomon was very wealthy. Solomon spoke of his riches in Ecclesiastes. Even Jesus referred to Solomon's riches. (Matthew 6:29)

37.) (Proverbs 28:27) d) give to the poor

38.) (Proverbs 29:22) c) stirs up even more anger

39.) Thirty-nine

? ? ? ? ? ? ? ? ?

1.) (Proverbs 31:10) a) virtuous

2.) A favorable character trait such as honesty, charity, thrift, or integrity; Christian behavior.

3.) (Proverbs 31:10) rubies

4.) (Proverbs 31:11) c) heart

5.) (Proverbs 31:13) wool and flax

6.) (Proverbs 31:28) her husband and children

7.) (Proverbs 31:13) c) works willingly

8.) (Proverbs 31:14) from far away

9.) (Proverbs 31:15) a) before dawn

10.) (Proverbs 31:14–19) willingness to work; the work ethic

11.) (Proverbs 31:20) d) charity

12.) (Proverbs 31:21) b) she has plenty of clothing to keep her family warm

13.) (Proverbs 31:22) purple

15.) (Proverbs 31:24) fine linen

16.) (Proverbs 31:25) d) strength and honor

17.) (Proverbs 31:26) wisdom

18.) (Proverbs 31:30) c) is not vain or conceited

19.) (Proverbs 31:30) fear of the Lord

20.) (Proverbs 31:30) She will be praised.

? ? ? ? ? ? ? ?

DREAM WEAVER

1.) Daniel

3.) (Daniel 1:8) d) to be excused from eating food forbidden under Jewish dietary laws

4.) (Daniel 1:9) favor and compassion

5.) (Daniel 1:17) understanding of visions and dreams

7.) (Daniel 2:12) that they all should be killed

8.) (Daniel 2:16–18) a) asked the king for more time and prayed to God for wisdom

9.) (Daniel 3:1) gold

11.) (Daniel 3:6) c) thrown into a fiery furnace

12.) (Daniel 4:32–33) a) went to live with the beasts of the field, eating grass for food

14.) (Daniel 5:4) He praised other gods.

15.) (Daniel 5:5) a) with handwriting on a wall

16.) (Daniel 5:12) Daniel

17.) (Daniel 5:10) the queen

18.) (Daniel 3:18) no

19.) (Daniel 3:25) God delivered them.

THE UNWILLING SERVANT

1.) Jonah

3.) (Jonah 1:2) Ninevah

4.) (Jonah 1:3) c) Joppa

5.) (Jonah 1:3) b) on a ship heading to Tarshish

7.) (Jonah 1:4) a great wind

8.) (Jonah 1:5) a) their gods

9.) (Jonah 1:12) d) throw him overboard

10.) (Jonah 1:13) No. They tried to row to land first, but failed because of the rough waters.

12.) (Jonah 1:15) d) grew calm

13.) (Jonah 2:1) He prayed.

14.) (Jonah 3:1–2) b) go to Ninevah

16.) (Jonah 1:17) three days and three nights

17.) (Jonah 3:4) that Ninevah would be overthrown in forty days

18.) (Jonah 3:5) a) fasted and wore sackcloth

19.) (Jonah 3:6) c) ashes

20.) (Jonah 3:10) He did not destroy them, but let them live.

22.) (Jonah 4:1) b) was angry

24.) (Jonah 4:5) to see what would happen to the city

25.) (Jonah 4:6) d) gourd

26.) (Jonah 4:9) angry

27.) (Jonah 4:10–11) that if he could feel pity for a plant, he should love the people living in Ninevah

29.) c) sixty-six books

? ? ? ? ? ? ? ? ?

1.) **Matthew**

3.) **d) Jesus' birth line, or genealogy**

5.) **(Matthew 2:1) Bethlehem**

7.) **(Matthew 2:13) d) kill Jesus**

8.) **(Matthew 2:13) a) Egypt**

9.) **(Matthew 3:4) d) locusts and wild honey**

11.) **(Matthew 4:2) forty days and forty nights**

12.) **(Matthew 4:19) men (or people)**

13.) **a) Beatitudes**

15.) **(Matthew 6:9–13) the Lord's Prayer**

16.) **(Matthew 6:20) d) heaven**

18.) (Matthew 7:12) the Golden Rule

19.) (Matthew 8:14) d) mother-in-law

20.) parables

21.) twelve

22.) (Matthew 14:26) a) ghost

23.) (Matthew 15:28) a) great faith

24.) (Matthew 20:17–19) yes

25.) (Matthew 24:42) b) we don't know
     when the Lord will return

26.) (Matthew 26:14–15) Judas Iscariot

27.) (Matthew 26:15) d) thirty pieces of
     silver

28.) (Matthew 26:36) the Garden of
     Gethsemane

? ? ? ? ? ? ? ? ?

29.) (Matthew 26:40, 43) a) slept

30.) (Matthew 26:48) b) kissing Him

31.) (Matthew 27:3) a) repented

32.) (Matthew 27:54) Truly this was the Son of God.

33.) (Matthew 28:2) d) an angel

34.) (Matthew 28:10) a) Galilee

35.) (Matthew 17:27) from the mouth of a fish

38.) (Matthew 28:11–15) They were bribed by the chief priests and elders to say that Jesus' disciples stole His body.

39.) That He is the Son of God.

40.) Amen.

JOHN'S JOURNEY WITH JESUS

1.) **John**

3.) **(John 2:1) c) Cana**

4.) **(John 2:3) His mother**

5.) **(John 2:1) c) wedding**

7.) **(John 2:15) d) overturned their tables and angrily rebuked them**

8.) **(John 3:16) b) eternal life**

9.) **(John 4:7) a drink of water**

10.) **(John 4:26) That He is the Messiah.**

11.) **(John 6:9) a) five barley loaves and two small fish**

12.) **(John 6:10) 5000**

13.) **(John 12:4) a) Judas Iscariot**

14.) (John 13:14) He washed their feet.

15.) (John 13:14) to serve one another

17.) (John 13:38) yes

18.) (John 18:27) c) rooster crowed

20.) (John 19:15) d) Crucify Him!

21.) (John 14:15) We will keep His commandments.

22.) (John 19:19) Jesus of Nazareth, King of the Jews

24.) (John 19:30) It is finished.

25.) (John 20:13) a) why weepest thou?

26.) (John 20:15) Woman, why weepest thou?

27.) (John 20:25) No. He wanted proof.

28.) (John 30:31) d) the Son of God, who is worthy to be worshiped

29.) (John 20:3I) d) believe in Jesus Christ, the Son of God, and have life in Jesus' name

30.) Amen.

? ? ? ? ? ? ? ?

1.) **Paul the Apostle**

2.) (Romans 1:7) **a) Roman Christians**

4.) (Romans 1:3) **d) Jesus Christ our Lord, the Son of God**

5.) (Romans 1:4) **Jesus' resurrection from the dead**

7.) (Romans 5:1) **d) faith in our Lord Jesus Christ**

8.) (Romans 5:18) **d) nothing. His gift of salvation is free.**

9.) (Romans 5:21) **Jesus Christ, the Son of God**

11.) (Hebrews 8:13) **a) the New Covenant**

12.) (Romans 8:1) **d) the Holy Spirit**

13.) (Romans 8:6) life and peace

14.) (Romans 3:10) no

15.) (Romans 8:26) The Holy Spirit tells God what the Christian needs.

16.) (Romans 8:27) b) God's

17.) (Romans 8:35–39) d) nothing

18.) (Romans 9:24) He means that the Gospel is for everyone, not just a certain group.

20.) (Romans 11:1) Benjamin

21.) (Romans 11:2) a) God has not forgotten His chosen people

22.) (Romans 11:13) c) Gentiles

? ? ? ? ? ? ? ? ?

23.) (Romans 11:13) the Gentiles

25.) (Romans 12:3–8) d) we should use whatever gifts God gave us

26.) (Romans 12:19) God

27.) (Romans 12:21) d) good

28.) (Romans 14:10) Jesus Christ

29.) (Romans 16:27) Amen.

? ? ? ? ? ? ? ? ?

1.) **Paul the Apostle**

2.) **b) Thessalonica**

4.) **(I Thessalonians 1:1) a) church**

6.) **(I Thessalonians 1:3) a) praises them**

7.) **(I Thessalonians 2:4) d) worry about pleasing God, not people**

8.) **(I Thessalonians 2:18) Satan**

10.) **(I Thessalonians 4:9) a) love one another**

11.) **(I Thessalonians 5:8) c) the breastplate of faith and love and a helmet of hope and salvation**

12.) **He told us to comfort each other.**

13.) **(I Thessalonians 5:17) to pray**

14.) **(I Thessalonians 5:22) a) evil**

15.) **d) Amen.**

HEBREWS

1.) We do not know, although some Bible scholars think Paul the Apostle wrote it.

3.) a) letter

4.) (Hebrews 1:1–2) d) through His Son Jesus

5.) (Hebrews 2:13) Jesus

6.) (Hebrews 5:8–9) eternal salvation; everlasting life

7.) (Hebrews 1:14) ministering spirits

8.) (Hebrews 4:16) b) mercy and grace

9.) (Hebrews 6:1) a) faith

10.) (Hebrews 6:10) He will not forget them.

12.) (Hebrews 11:6) d) faith

13.) (Hebrews 11) Abel, Enoch, Noah,
Abraham, Sarah, Isaac, Jacob, Joseph,
the parents of Moses, Moses, Rahab

14.) (Hebrews 12:2) He sits at the right
hand of the throne of God.

15.) Amen.

16.) (Hebrews 13:15) continual praise

17.) (Hebrews 12:10) c) wants us to learn
how to be holy

18.) (Hebrews 12:14) d) holiness

19.) (Hebrews 13:2) a) angels

? ? ? ? ? ? ? ?

20.) (Hebrews 13:8–9) We should ignore strange teachings because any teaching about God that does not come from the Bible is false. Jesus Christ never changes. His Word stays the same.

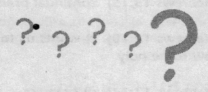

JOHN'S LETTERS

1.) A letter

2.) three

3.) d) John the Apostle

4.) (I John 1:8) a) ourselves

6.) (I John 3:11) that we should love one another

7.) (I John 4:9) a) sent His only begotten Son into the world, that we might live through Him

8.) (I John 2:15) d) the world

9.) (I John 2:5) a) love

10.) (I John 4:8) God is Love.

11.) (I John 4:15) God will live in them, and they will live in God.

12.) (I John 4:21) People who love God love their brother.

14.) (I John 5:21) d) idols

15.) Amen

17.) (2 John 1:3) grace, mercy, and peace

18.) (2 John 1:7–10) a) not let the person into your house

19.) (2 John 1:11) Because if you do, you will be just as bad as the false Christian.

20.) (2 John 1:12) Because he hopes to see his readers in person soon.

21.) d) Amen.

23.) (3 John 1:2) John wished Gaius prosperity and health.

24.) (3 John 1:3) a) a strong Christian who walked in the truth

25) (3 John 1:9) a) was more concerned
about his reputation than he was about
other Christians

26.) (3 John:11) people who do evil

27.) (3 John 1:11) good

28.) (3 John 1:12) c) was a true Christian
witness

29.) (3 John 1:13–14) d) hoped to see
them in person soon

30.) (3 John 1:14) peace

? ? ? ? ? ? ? ?

1.) Jude

3.) (Jude 1:1) a) Christians in the early church

4.) (Jude 1:2) mercy, peace, and love

5.) (Jude 1:4) b) denied our Lord God and His Son Jesus Christ

6.) (Jude 1:7) Sodom and Gomorrah

7.) (Jude 1:11) b) Cain

8.) (Jude 1:16) d) will say nice things they don't mean to important people who can help them

9.) Proverbs

10.) (Jude 1:25) Amen

11.) (Jude 1:18) a) are more interested in worldly things like being rich and popular than in God

12.) (Jude 1:20) They can pray in the Holy Spirit.

13.) (Jude 1:21) d) in God's love

14.) (Jude 1:21) eternal life

15.) (Jude 1:25) God

SUPER BIBLE ACTIVITIES FOR KIDS!

Barbour's Super Bible Activity Books, packed with fun illustrations and kid-friendly text, will appeal to children ages six to twelve. And the price—only $1.39—will appeal to parents. All books are paperbound. The unique size (4⅛" x 5⅜") makes these books easy to take anywhere!

A Great Selection to Satisfy All Kids!

Bible Activities	*Fun Bible Trivia 2*
Bible Activities for Kids	*Great Bible Trivia for Kids*
Bible Connect the Dots	*More Bible Activities*
Bible Crosswords for Kids	*More Bible Crosswords for Kids*
Bible Picture Fun	*More Clean Jokes for Kids*
Bible Word Games	*Super Bible Activities*
Bible Word Searches for Kids	*Super Bible Crosswords*
Clean Jokes for Kids	*Super Bible Word Searches*
Fun Bible Trivia	*Super Silly Stories*